PEACE IN THE VALLEY

21 Days of Finding Light in the Darkest Hour

Deb Preston

BRIGHTER SIDE
PUBLISHING

To Josh.

Table of Contents

Introduction

To the person who's not sure how much longer they can go on like this...

To the one who's been holding on for what feels like an eternity, just waiting for something. Anything. Searching for hope...

To the one whose hope hasn't come, whose every day bleeds into the next as the light slips further and further from sight...

To you, in the dark:

This is not how your story ends.

It's not.

Because arching over your darkest night, and over your brightest day, over the whole of your life and all of eternity, is a holy God. He is in control. And He does not abandon His children to die in the dark.

No matter how hopeless it looks right now, God promises, "I know what I'm doing. I have it all planned out—plans to take care of you, not abandon you, plans to give you the future you hope for" (Jeremiah 29:11).

And His plans will always prevail (Proverbs 19:21).

So don't lose hope.

Don't lose sight of God's promises.

In reading this book, take one day at a time. Read one chapter and find just one truth to mull over each day.

Think about it. Pray about it. And come back the next day for one more chapter, one more truth, one more story about one more escape route from rock bottom.

Trust God. Lean your full weight on Him. Your God has a reputation for spectacular rescues. And He will not disappoint.

DAY 1

THE ISRAELITES
IN THE WILDERNESS

God will help you deal with whatever hard things
come up when the time comes.
—Matthew 6:34—

Everyone knows the story of the Israelites being rescued from slavery in Egypt. It's a Sunday School favorite.

God sent ten different plagues to convince Pharaoh to release them and even compelled the Egyptians to send the Israelites off with gifts—livestock, clothing, silver, and gold! When Pharaoh changed his mind and chased after

3

them, God parted the Red Sea so the Israelites could pass through to safety and freedom.

They were probably feeling high on life! They were rescued from hard lives of slavery, loaded down with gifts, and on a short journey to the Promised Land. Scholars predict that the journey should have taken them *11 days.*

And then just three days into their journey, they couldn't find water, then it was food. Then an 11-day journey turned into a month, and then a year, and then *40 years.*

Have you been there? You feel like you've been walking through the valley forever? Can't even remember the last time you weren't struggling?

The Israelites had seen God perform incredible miracles! Why wouldn't He just do it again and place them safely in the Promised Land?

But if you look a little closer, you'll see that God *did* supply their every need. He provided water (Exodus 15:22-25, 17:1-7) and manna (16:1-18) but only provided "each day's ration" (16:4). And He went ahead of them in a Pillar of Cloud and Fire, to guide them each day.

When we're in the valley, we want incredible miracles, don't we? We want to arrive in the Promised Land as quickly as possible and we want to know the timeline for getting there.

However, God never promised us a detailed itinerary, or even an efficient one. Jesus encouraged us in Matthew 6:33-34 (emphasis added):

4

"Don't worry about missing out. You'll find all your everyday human concerns will be met. *Give your entire attention to what God is doing right now,* and don't get worked up about what may or may not happen tomorrow. God will help you deal with whatever hard things come up when the time comes."

When God sent manna to the Israelites and explained that they would be receiving their rations just one day at a time, He told Moses, "I'm going to test them to see if they'll live according to my teaching or not" (Exodus 16:4).

God lead 600,000 Israelite men out of Egypt. If they were each married with just one child, that would make roughly 1,800,000 Israelites wandering through the desert.

Do you know how many survived the wilderness of those original 1,800,000? Just two—Joshua and Caleb.

Joshua and Caleb accepted their daily rations of food and direction with grateful hearts and trusted God to supply every need in due time. *They gave their entire attention to what God was doing in each moment.*

The Holy Spirit encourages us in Hebrews 3:7-9, "Today, please listen; don't turn a deaf ear as in 'the bitter uprising,' that time of wilderness testing! Even though they watched me at work for forty years, your ancestors refused to let me do it my way."

How do you respond when you don't know the future? When you can't see the light at the end of the tunnel?

I'm a Type A personality. I'm booking hotels months in advance, babysitters weeks in advance, and making plans for how I'll spend each day, days in advance.

Why? I'm more comfortable when life is predictable, when I know exactly what to expect and when.

But even us Type As can lean into God's promise in Jeremiah 29:11, "I know what I'm doing. I have it all planned out—plans to take care of you, not abandon you, plans to give you the future you hope for."

Write this verse down. Read it until you memorize it. And say it out loud until you believe it with every fiber of your being. You can lean into God's promises.

God has good plans for you, plans to take care of you, to give you the future you hope for. But He might supply your every need just one day at a time.

Hang in there. Let's take this journey together, one day, one step at a time. Think about these words, pray about them, and come back tomorrow for your next daily ration.

DAVID

Summing it all up, friends, I'd say you'll do best by
filling your minds and meditating on things true,
noble, reputable, authentic, compelling, gracious—
the best, not the worst; the beautiful, not the ugly;
things to praise, not things to curse.
—Philippians 4:8—

We all know the story of David and Goliath (1 Samuel
17:1-54) and how David was selected from among all of his
older, stronger brothers to be the king of Israel (1 Samuel
16:1-13). But did you know that after David was anointed

as the next king, Saul (the current king) hunted him endlessly, trying to kill him?

David did nothing but honor and serve Saul faithfully. In return Saul, fueled by jealousy and fear, cheated David out of a wife, labeled him an outlaw, tried to kill him, and even murdered the priests who dared to help him. David was forced to live on the run for seven years, hiding in desert caves, always looking over his shoulder.

No one would have blamed David if he had fought back. In fact, he was given two clear opportunities to kill Saul and end the chase once and for all (1 Samuel 24, 26). Both times he refrained, saying in 1 Samuel 24:12-13:

> "God may avenge me, but it is in His hands, not mine. An old proverb says, 'Evil deeds come from evil people.' So be assured that my hand won't touch you."

David determined that no matter what anyone else did, *he* would live an exemplary life. And that his life would speak for itself, acting as an undeniable witness to his character.

How did David manage to maintain this attitude in the face of such adversity? The answer may be hidden in the psalms.

The book of Psalms, written by David, is full of David crying out to God about his circumstances, begging him for help and intervention. "I cry out loudly to God, loudly I plead with God for mercy. I spill out all my complaints before Him, and spell out my troubles in detail" (Psalm 142:1-2).

But nearly every cry for help is followed by praise. "I'll bless you every day, and keep it up from now to eternity" (Psalm 145:2).

David acknowledged his pain and his walk through the valley but he didn't stay there in his heart, did he? After he wept before God, he praised God. He made a conscious decision to praise God, to dwell on *God's goodness* rather than on the details of his current situation.

It reminds me of Philippians 4:8, which urges us, "Summing it all up, friends, I'd say you'll do best by filling your minds and meditating on things true, noble, reputable, authentic, compelling, gracious—the best, not the worst; the beautiful, not the ugly; things to praise, not things to curse."

Likewise, Martin Luther once said, "You can't keep the birds from flying over your head but you can prevent them from building a nest in your hair." He was referring to sinful thoughts but the same could be said for negative thoughts.

We'll inevitably grieve time spent in the valley, but we *must* stop ourselves from becoming consumed by our grief and negative thoughts. In making a conscious decision to praise God in spite of negative circumstances, we can help ourselves to keep our eyes focused on God through all of it.

So what are you dwelling on today? Make the decision, right now, to turn the tables and dwell on God's goodness.

Remember what He's done for you in the past and what He's done for others. No matter what our current circumstances, He is always worthy of praise.

JUDAH IN BABYLONIAN EXILE

Live and obey and love and believe right there. God, not your circumstances, defines your life.

—1 Corinthians 7:17—

In 2 Kings 24, King Nebuchadnezzar led the Babylonian army against the people of Judah. They destroyed the temple, left Jerusalem in ruins, and took thousands captive to Babylon. Those left behind in Jerusalem were no better off, poor and oppressed by both Babylonians and neighboring nations.

False prophets preached hope to the exiles, assuring

them that victory and return to their home country was just around the corner. So they waited…and waited…and waited. Their victory didn't arrive at the falsely prophesied time, but a whopping *70 years* later.

Have you been there? Everyone around you is reassuring you that your time is coming, the end of your hard times is just around the corner. So you keep waiting… and waiting…and waiting. The longer we're in the valley, the harder it is to maintain our hope, isn't it?

God spoke the truth to the prophet Jeremiah, and it wasn't what the people were hoping to hear.

> "As soon as Babylon's seventy years are up and not a day before, I'll show up and take care of you as I promised and bring you back home. I know what I'm doing. I have it all planned out—plans to take care of you, not abandon you, plans to give you the future you hope for" (Jeremiah 29:10-11).

We read those words just a few days ago. But did you realize the "future you hope for" would only arrive in "seventy years…and not a day before"?

Depressing? A little.

So what should they do in the meantime? While they waited for their victory? God advised them in Jeremiah 29:5-7 to make the best of it.

> "Build houses and make yourselves at home. Put in gardens and eat what grows in that country. Marry

and have children. Encourage your children to marry and have children so that you'll thrive in that country and not waste away. Make yourselves at home there and work for the country's welfare. Pray for Babylon's well-being. If things go well for Babylon, things will go well for you."

They couldn't and shouldn't stop *living* because they were in captivity. It reminds me of Paul's advice to those in less-than-ideal marriages in 1 Corinthians 7:17:

> And don't be wishing you were someplace else or with someone else. Where you are right now is God's place for you. Live and obey and love and believe right there. God, not your marital status, defines your life.

We could replace "marital status" with a lot of different statuses.

God, not your health status, defines your life.

God, not your job status, defines your life.

God, not your financial status, defines your life.

That's not to say that "God's place for you" is necessarily in a valley of pain and suffering but that God has called us to obedient living no matter what our circumstances. We're to keep living, to make the best of things, and to "live and obey and love and believe right there."

God was absolutely true to His promise to the Judean

exiles and He'll be true to His promise to you. No matter what circumstances you're facing in the meantime, remember that God, not your circumstances, defines your life. So "live and obey and love and believe" right where you are.

JOSEPH

Sometimes when you're in a dark place you think
you've been buried but you've actually been planted.
—Christine Caine—

Ever feel like you just can't win? Like every single
thing that *could* go wrong, *does*?

Joseph knew that feeling! His own brothers sold him
into slavery.

He was purchased by one of Pharaoh's officials. Things
were starting to look up! But then he refused the advances

of his master's wife, so she falsely accused him of coming on to her and had him thrown him in jail.

While in jail, Joseph interpreted a dream for Pharaoh's cupbearer and asked him to return the favor by facilitating his release from prison. But the cupbearer didn't hold up his end of the deal.

For years, Joseph did nothing but serve God and others faithfully. He did absolutely nothing to deserve the hand he was dealt.

He might have wondered if God was angry with him or had forgotten him. But God assures us in Isaiah 49:15, "Can a mother forget the infant at her breast, walk away from the baby she bore? But even if mothers forget, I'd never forget you—never."

God didn't forget Joseph. He gave Pharaoh a dream and the *only person* He gave the interpretation to, was Joseph.

Joseph left a jail cell, where he might have assumed no one even knew he was alive, and walked straight into the presence of a *king*, the Pharaoh. He interpreted Pharaoh's dream that warned of seven years of famine on the way.

Pharaoh was so impressed by Joseph that he put him in charge of famine preparations, in charge of the entire country in fact. He was second only to Pharaoh himself!

And God blessed Joseph with the wisdom he needed in his new position. The Bible reports that "all countries experienced famine; Egypt was the only country that had bread" (Genesis 41:54).

Soon his own brothers, the same ones who sold him

into slavery, traveled to Egypt in search of food. Did Joseph kill them on the spot? Sell *them* off as slaves?

No. He revealed his identity and told them in Genesis 45:5-8:

> "Don't feel badly, don't blame yourselves for selling me. God was behind it. God sent me here ahead of you to save lives. There has been a famine in the land now for two years; the famine will continue for five more years—neither plowing nor harvesting. God sent me on ahead to pave the way and make sure there was a remnant in the land, to save your lives in an amazing act of deliverance. So you see, it wasn't *you* who sent me here but *God*. He set me in place as a father to Pharaoh, put me in charge of his personal affairs, and made me ruler of all Egypt" (emphasis added).

You see, Joseph knew that if he hadn't been sold into slavery, he would have never lived in Egypt. If he hadn't been falsely accused by the wife of Pharaoh's official, he wouldn't have been thrown into the jail of the king's prisoners. And if he wasn't in *that* jail, he would have never befriended the Pharaoh's cupbearer, who later brought him into the presence of Pharaoh.

Are you really cursed? Or is God lining up the pieces to help you arrive at your God-appointed destiny? To place you in a position to save lives?

Although it *appeared* as if God had thrown Joseph into a

life of slavery, He was actually divinely positioning him to place him over an entire country, second only to a king.

I love a quote by author Christine Caine. She says, "Sometimes when you're in a dark place you think you've been buried but you've actually been planted."

They feel the same, being buried and being planted. But Romans 8:28 reminds us, "every detail in our lives of love for God is worked into something good."

God is in the business of planting, not burying. So don't lose hope! When we hold tightly to God's promises, when we trust that He does what He says He will, we're digging up through the dirt and darkness to burst forth into the light.

Your time is coming. Keep digging.

NAOMI

Therefore, prophesy.
—Ezekiel 37:12—

In the book of Ruth, we meet Naomi. She left her hometown with her husband and sons to live in the country of Moab. But her husband passed away there, followed by both of her sons a few years later, leaving Naomi and her Moabite daughters-in-law alone in the middle of a famine.

Naomi heard there was food in her hometown of Bethlehem, so she returned there with her widowed daughter-in-law, Ruth. Can you imagine returning to your hometown, everyone eager to hear what you've been up to all this time, with no husband, no children, and no hope after so much loss?

She told the people in Ruth 1:20-21:

> "Don't call me Naomi; call me Bitter. The Strong One has dealt me a bitter blow. I left here full of life, and God has brought me back with nothing but the clothes on my back. Why would you call me Naomi? God certainly doesn't. The Strong One ruined me."

Soon after their return, Ruth set out to follow some harvesters, collecting their leftover grains from the field. Of all the fields she might have chosen, she happened to wander into the field of Boaz, a close relative of Naomi's husband. She found extreme favor with him and was given food, special treatment, and an invitation to continue working in his fields.

When Naomi heard the news, she told Ruth, "God hasn't quite walked out on us after all! He still loves us, in bad times as well as good" (Ruth 2:20). You see, even when Naomi was *convinced* that God had it out for her and told anyone who would listen, God was *still* present, working things out for her good.

Ruth eventually married Boaz and had a son, Obed. Naomi loved him dearly and was brought back to such life and vitality by his birth, that people began to refer to Obed as "Naomi's baby boy."

He became the father of Jesse, who became the father of King David. And generations later, *Jesus* was born into the family line.

Do you sometimes feel like you've lost too much for your life to be redeemed and made whole again? Naomi even rejected her own name, which meant "pleasant," because it felt like a lie. She asked people to call her Bitter instead.

But did you ever notice that in spite of her request, she's *not* referred to as "Bitter" in the entire book of Ruth? Because despite her emotions and outlook on her future, her *actual* future *was* pleasant. The death of her husband and children was not the end of her story and the writer of the book knew that.

It reminds me of something I read recently in Ezekiel. God took the prophet Ezekiel to a field full of dry bones and asked him in Ezekiel 37:3, "Son of man, can these bones live?"

Now obviously, humanly, dry bones cannot live again. They're done. Who could possibly put them back together and bring them to life again? But Ezekiel, despite his human perspective, answered, "Master God, only you know that."

God told Ezekiel to prophesy over the bones, to speak the message of God to them. And the bones responded, coming together, skin forming and stretching over them, and then breath entering them and bringing them alive again.

And then? My favorite part in verses 11-14:

> Then God said to me, "Son of man, these bones are the whole house of Israel. Listen to what they're saying: 'Our bones are dried up, our hope is gone, there's nothing left of us.'

> Therefore, prophesy. Tell them, 'God, the Master, says: I'll dig up your graves and bring you out alive —O my people! Then I'll take you straight to the land of Israel. When I dig up graves and bring you out as my people, you'll realize that I am God...I've said it and I'll do it. God's Decree.'"

You are not done. You are not "Bitter." You may look dead, you may even feel dead, but that doesn't stop your Creator for a second.

So like Ezekiel, speak God's truth over your life. Speak "pleasant." Speak God's message from Jeremiah 29:11, "I know what I'm doing. I have it all planned out—plans to take care of you, not abandon you, plans to give you the future you hope for."

Hear the word of the Lord. Speak it. Shout it over the lies of the enemy.

Rise up, dry bones! This is not how your story ends.

THE PERSISTENT WIDOW

Jesus told them a story showing that it was
necessary for them to pray consistently and never
quit.
—Luke 18:1—

Have you heard Jesus' story of the persistent widow? It's so short that it's easy to miss in the book of Luke.

In it, a widow's rights are being violated but the judge that *could* help her "never gave God a thought and cared nothing for people" (Luke 18:2). Regardless of this fact, the widow persisted in her pleas.

The judge cared nothing for justice and saw her persistence purely as a nuisance. *But* he finally gave in and helped her, if only to get her off his case.

Jesus sums up the story in verses 6-8 by saying:

> "Do you hear what that judge, corrupt as he is, is saying? So what makes you think God won't step in and work justice for his chosen people, who continue to cry out for help? Won't he stick up for them? I assure you, he will. He will not drag his feet. But how much of that kind of persistent faith will the Son of Man find on the earth when he returns?"

I used to think that prayer was a one-and-done type of thing. I mean, obviously God knows my needs. I've already told Him, so why would I keep bringing it up day after day?

Because in verse one, before the story is even told, we're informed, "Jesus told them a story showing that *it was necessary for them to pray consistently and never quit.*" Ephesians 6:18 agrees, instructing us to "always keep on praying."

I read something by missionary Samuel Isenhower that really struck me. He said, "God takes your prayers as seriously as you take them."

I can understand this from my perspective as a parent. If my daughter tells me she wants something in passing but then never mentions it again, I won't usually give it to her. If she doesn't care about it enough to persist in her requests, then I'll save my time, money, and energy for something she's more passionate about.

It's not that God has limited time or money or energy but that He specifically instructed us through the parable in Luke to pray *with persistence* and to build our faith in doing so.

Another requirement of our prayers is that they *must* be sincere. How can we know if they're truly sincere? Isenhower proposes that we must be willing to be part of the answer. He writes:

> Can I pray sincerely, "Lord, improve my marriage" if I have no intention to treat my wife any differently? Can I ask sincerely, "Lord, unite your church" if I still hold onto unforgiveness? Can I petition, "God, bring revival to this city" if I'm not actively trying to talk with people and lead them to Christ? If I don't want it bad enough for it to change my external life, then it means that in my prayer I'm just pretending.

What does that mean for our prayers when we're in the valley? Well, we can't pray for a spouse's salvation but never talk with them about Jesus. We can't pray for a better job but then knowingly do shoddy work at the job we have.

God doesn't expect us to simply become the answer to our own prayers but we must be willing to move our feet in that direction.

Pray persistently. Pray sincerely. God will meet you there.

JOB

I know that my redeemer lives, and that in the end he
will stand on the earth.
—Job 19:25—

Have you heard the story of Job? In one afternoon, he
lost *all ten* of his children and all of his wealth. Just a few
days later, he was struck with a disease that left him
covered in ulcers and scabs from head to toe.

Three of his friends came to visit and comfort him. And
nearly the entire book of Job recounts their conversation,

debating as to why Job was suffering and what part God plays in our suffering.

Though Job's initial reaction to tragedy was faithfulness, his resolve began to fade as more time passed without healing. And I can certainly understand that.

He cursed the day he was born, and questioned in Job 3:20-23:

> "Why does God bother giving light to the miserable, why bother keeping bitter people alive, those who want in the worst way to die, and can't, who can't imagine anything better than death, who count the day of their death and burial the happiest day of their life? What's the point of life when it doesn't make sense, when God blocks all the roads to meaning?"

Job was convinced it would have been better if he had never been born. His friends apparently felt the moment Job longed for death was the best time to attack him, insisting that *truly* good people don't experience suffering. Their accusations led Job to pray in 13:20-24:

> "Please, God, I have two requests; grant them so I'll know I count with you: First, lay off the afflictions; the terror is too much for me. Second, address me directly so I can answer you, or let me speak and then you answer me. How many sins have been charged against me? Show me the list—how bad is

it? Why do you stay hidden and silent? Why treat me like I'm your enemy?"

Have you ever prayed that? Or wished for it? A chance to speak with God directly about your trials, to ask what you've done to deserve them?

I believe God might have allowed Job to suffer so that we could all connect with him. Because so very many of us have been in this exact place. We think we'd be better off dead. We don't understand why we've experienced so much darkness and suffering.

Throughout the book, we see that Job questioned God but he didn't stay there forever. In chapter ten, he longs for death as the end of everything.

In chapter fourteen, he still longs for death but then turns a corner, asking God, "If someone dies, will they live again? All the days of my hard service I will wait for my renewal to come" (Job 14:14). It seems he's gaining a new perspective.

Finally he finds his answer in Job 19:25, "I know that my redeemer lives, and that in the end he will stand on the earth." No, he still doesn't understand why good people suffer but he rests in the fact that he's limited by his human perspective.

At the end of the book of Job, God answers Job from the eye of a violent storm. He asks Job questions about the forming of the world and everything within it, and asks if Job is prepared and able to fill God's shoes.

God opens Job's eyes to see that he is utterly

surrounded by mystery. He cannot comprehend it all and so cannot understand God's working at times. But he can trust that God is sovereign and that everything He does is right and good.

We may not understand it all now but that's okay. One day, we will. We'll be able to look back and see God's hand moving in *everything*, good or bad, working it *all* together for the good of those who love Him (Romans 8:28).

MOSES

Pile your troubles on God's shoulders—he'll carry
your load, he'll help you out.
—Psalm 55:22—

Moses?! Why is Moses in this book on valleys and suffering? He brought down the plagues, parted the Red Sea, and received the Ten Commandments directly from God. His life was essentially one highlight reel after another!

Ah, but it wasn't. He spent one-third of his life wandering the desert.

Now despite Moses' limitations, he had trusted God to use him to speak to Pharaoh and deliver the people of Israel from slavery. And God made good on His promise! Miracle after miracle proved God's power and faithfulness.

Remember when we learned a few days ago that the 40-year journey to the Promised Land should have only taken 11 days? Why did the journey take so long? The Bible says in Exodus 13:17, "It so happened that after Pharaoh released the people, God didn't lead them by the road through the land of the Philistines, which was the shortest route, for God thought, 'If the people encounter war, they'll change their minds and go back to Egypt.'"

So already, the journey is taking longer because even after all of God's mighty miracles, the Israelites were afraid. Not a great start.

And then just *three days* into their journey, the complaining started. First, it was water, then it was food.

God miraculously provided their every need but leave it to the Israelites to find a reason to complain. "We don't want manna, we want meat! And we want more variety on the menu!" Siiiiigh.

Then, as the Israelites are literally following their God in a cloud of *fire* to the Promised Land, drinking water from stones and eating bread from heaven, they're experimenting with other gods, worshipping idols made of wood and metal.

Can you imagine being Moses? You know what God is capable of, you trust Him to do what He says, and here you are...herding cats to the Promised Land.

The people you're in charge of don't trust God despite miracle after miracle being performed for their benefit. They complained and rebelled and nagged Moses so much that he asked God to kill him in an act of mercy! Did you know that?

> Moses said to God, "Why are you treating me this way? What did I ever do to you to deserve this? Did I conceive them? Was I their mother? So why dump the responsibility of this people on me? Why tell me to carry them around like a nursing mother, carry them all the way to the land you promised to their ancestors? Where am I supposed to get meat for all these people who are whining to me, 'Give us meat; we want meat.' I can't do this by myself— it's too much, all these people. If this is how you intend to treat me, do me a favor and kill me. I've seen enough; I've had enough. Let me out of here" (Numbers 11:11-15).

Have you ever felt that way? So utterly exhausted? So pushed to the limits of your human abilities that death sounded appealing? Instead of granting his request, God provided relief by anointing other leaders to help Moses carry the burden.

See, the Israelites were out to have their needs met. And if God wasn't fast enough, they'd find what they needed elsewhere.

But Moses looked to *God* to meet every need. He

wasn't chasing temporary highs. He was willing to wait on the real thing, on a complete and *lasting* solution.

We read the stories and shake our heads at the Israelites. I mean, how could they have gotten so far off track in their faith, am I right?

But...have you ever looked to your spouse to meet your emotional needs? To complete you? Or counted on your friends to fend off your loneliness?

And who do you call first with your problems? Your mom? Your best friend? God is often second, third, or even last on our list.

Have you found comfort in food or alcohol when God didn't calm your nerves quickly enough? Do you feel a high from the approval of social media likes, friends, or followers? Have you placed emotional stock in others' approval of your talent, career, or appearance?

There are two huge problems with these worldly solutions. First of all, as Christians we've been called to bring every need to God, including our needs for emotional support, empathy, comfort, peace, acceptance, approval, fulfillment, and more. Secondly, anything the world has to offer, even our human relationships, are only temporary fixes and will never fully and permanently satisfy our needs.

See, the world is full of God-substitutes, quick fixes when we're tired of waiting on God to meet our needs. They look different than the fixes the Israelites used but they're serving the same purpose.

MOSES

Instead of seeking alternative solutions, Moses brought *every* need to God and trusted God to meet him there. And He did. Every. single. time.

Wait on God today. He's the only one with a real and lasting solution to what you're facing. Bring every need before Him.

He's listening. He'll fight your battles.

JESUS

But please, not what I want. What do you want?
—Luke 22:42—

There's a meme making its rounds on the internet. It shows Mel Gibson, who directed *The Passion of the Christ*, sitting with the actor who portrayed Jesus as they appear to discuss a scene.

"Jesus" is wearing a thorn of crowns and covered in blood. The caption reads, "That moment when you try to explain to Jesus how hard your life has been lately."

It's just a funny meme, not meant to downplay anyone's situation, but it makes a valid point. Jesus lived a pretty miserable life if you think about it.

His own brothers and hometown neighbors questioned His deity. He was constantly attacked by religious leaders, determined to either throw Him in jail or kill Him. He couldn't get a second to Himself before crowds overtook Him and the majority of the people in His life weren't there to support Him but to ask, "What's in it for me?"

At the time He needed His friends most, they abandoned him. He cried out to God, His Father, with no answer or relief and then was tortured and killed on a cross, bearing the weight of the sins of the *entire world* on His shoulders.

If anyone has been there, done that, leading a difficult life, it was Jesus. Hebrews 4:15 reminds us of Jesus, our priest, "We don't have a priest who is out of touch with our reality. He's been through weakness and testing, experienced it all—all but the sin."

How did Jesus approach suffering and rejection? We have to start by considering Jesus' purposes on earth, stated by Scripture. He was here to seek and save the lost (Luke 19:10), destroy the works of the devil (1 John 3:8), do the will of God who sent Him (John 6:38), serve (Mark 10:45), and save (John 6:40).

Jesus was always, always, *always* focused on His purposes here on earth. He came straight from heaven, knew God, was God, and knew how fleeting life here on earth is.

He wasn't swayed from His purpose by rejection, abandonment, or persecution, because He had seen it all a million times and knew that there was something greater in store, Some*one* greater in control. He could see beyond the price He had to pay, to focus on the sweet and glorious outcome of His suffering.

Of course, Jesus didn't *want* to die a torturous death on the cross. Who would? Luke 22:41-44 tells us:

> He pulled away from them about a stone's throw, knelt down, and prayed, "Father, remove this cup from me. But please, not what I want. What do you want?" At once an angel from heaven was at his side, strengthening him. He prayed on all the harder. Sweat, wrung from him like drops of blood, poured off his face.

Jesus asked God to save Him from suffering but immediately shifted His prayer back to His purpose—"What do *you* want, God?"

To be frank, I find this chapter, these thoughts, to be the most challenging for me personally. I've recently been studying the purposes of Jesus on earth. After all, if we are "Christians," we are to be as Christ-like as possible. And while Jesus' purposes—to seek and save the lost, destroy the works of the devil, do the will of God who sent Him, serve, and save—sound appropriate for my life, my actions don't always reflect these purposes.

I think the most challenging part of being a follower of

Christ is keeping your eyes on eternity. We know in our *heads* that earth is not our home but most of us don't *truly* know it in our hearts.

If we did, I don't think we'd worry as much. I doubt we'd invest so much time, energy, and money into meaningless things. I think we'd treat people a lot differently.

But how in the world do you convince yourself of God's ultimate reign and control and greater purposes, and then *keep* your mind and heart focused there? For me, it's about reading and rereading and memorizing Scripture.

Did you know that God designed our brains so that the more we think about something, the more we say something out loud, the more likely we are to default to that way of thinking naturally? I believe that's a huge reason there are countless Bible verses about the power of words. They're literally life-changing.

So I spend the first part of every day reading God's Word, the Bible. From stories in the Old Testament to Psalms of praise to teachings in the New Testament, I can see how everything centers on and comes back to God's sovereign power over all eternity. I'm reminded in a hundred different ways that this world is not my home and that God is doing something greater than these silly details on which we waste so much of our hearts.

I also make an effort to focus the majority of my music listening on uplifting Christian songs. It's easy to get caught up in a wealth and sex culture when that's the message you're constantly feeding your brain. But when I'm continuously listening to lyrics that say "there is no one like our God," and "great is Your faithfulness, You've never failed me yet," you'd better believe they take root in my heart. Those words come back to me when I need them most, when I need the reminder the most.

Philippians 4:8 encourages us, "Summing it all up, friends, I'd say you'll do best by filling your minds and meditating on things true, noble, reputable, authentic, compelling, gracious—the best, not the worst; the beautiful, not the ugly; things to praise, not things to curse."

So focus on eternity today. Think on it...and then think on it again.

Hold up every word you say, every action you take, and ask yourself if it lines up with the purposes of Jesus on earth. And as you focus on eternity, I pray that "the things of earth will grow strangely dim in the light of His glory and grace."

DANIEL

They defeated him through the blood of the Lamb
and the bold word of their witness.
—Revelation 12:11—

Have you ever served someone faithfully, blessing them for years, only to have them feed you to lions? No? Well, Daniel is rolling over in his grave somewhere, sighing, "Story of my life!"

His hometown of Jerusalem was attacked and he, along with other promising young men, was exiled to Babylon to be trained for service in the Babylonian king's court. God blessed Daniel there, gifting him and causing him to stand out from the others.

When God enabled him to interpret a mysterious dream for King Nebuchadnezzar, the king promoted Daniel to governor of Babylon and chief over all of the Babylonian wise men. But, as in so many of the stories in this book, God's blessing on Daniel made others jealous. The Bible tells us that they tried to find an old scandal in Daniel's life, a skeleton to drag out of his closet, but they couldn't find a thing.

The one thing they did know was that Daniel served God faithfully. So they convinced the king to issue a decree that every person should pray to the king alone for the next 30 days and that anyone who prayed to any other god would be thrown into the lions' den.

But Daniel refused to hide or downplay his beliefs. He continued to pray to God and was caught in the act.

The king tried to get Daniel out of it. He loved him! But his decree could not be reversed.

So he placed Daniel in the lions' den, assuring him, "Your God, to whom you are so loyal, is going to get you out of this" (Daniel 6:16). The king didn't even serve or worship God but couldn't deny His power at work in Daniel's life. Oh, that we would *all* live out that kind of faith!

And sure enough, when the king ran to the den the next morning, he found Daniel alive, not a scratch on him. Daniel told the king in Daniel 6:21-22:

"My God sent his angel, who closed the mouths of the lions so that they would not hurt me. I've been found innocent before God and also before you, O king. I've done nothing to harm you."

The king was so impressed that he issued a new decree, that every person should pray to God alone. *An entire country* began to serve and worship God because of Daniel's unapologetic faith.

Perhaps you're surrounded by lions today. Maybe your circumstances are pressing in around you, circling you, keeping you up at night. The incredible news is that the God of Daniel is our God too, and He's the same yesterday, today, and forever.

Lions may circle you, troubling waters may try to drown you, but hold tight to your faith! Tie yourself into a life of obedience to, and unapologetic worship of, God.

When we're delivered from these circumstances (and we will be!), our *test* will become a *testimony* to others. Even those who don't believe in God won't be able to deny His power at work in our lives.

How many believers will be encouraged in their faith by your testimony? How many nonbelievers will come to know and worship God because of it?

Only God knows now but you'll know soon enough. You'll see it with your own eyes. You just have to hold on in this lions' den until the morning finally arrives.

SHADRACH, MESHACH, AND ABEDNEGO

I, your God, have a firm grip on you and I'm not
letting go. I'm telling you, "Don't panic. I'm right here
to help you."
—Isaiah 41:13—

Daniel wasn't the only one exiled to Babylon to be
trained for service in the Babylonian king's court.
Shadrach, Meshach, and Abednego experienced this same
fate. They were blessed by God alongside Daniel and
when Daniel was promoted to governor of Babylon, these

three were appointed to administrative posts at Daniel's request.

But it wasn't long before King Nebuchadnezzar built a gold statue, ninety feet high and nine feet thick. This was serious work on his part—it wasn't a small undertaking to build a statue nine stories tall in (very roughly) 550 BC.

He commanded that everyone bow down and worship the statue or else risk being thrown into a roaring furnace. But Shadrach, Meshach, and Abednego refused to worship the statue.

King Nebuchadnezzar was furious, asking them in Daniel 3:15, "Who is the god who can rescue you from my power?" And *man*, do I love their response in 3:16-18:

> Shadrach, Meshach, and Abednego answered King Nebuchadnezzar, "Your threat means nothing to us. If you throw us in the fire, the God we serve can rescue us from your roaring furnace and anything else you might cook up, O king. But even if he doesn't, it wouldn't make a bit of difference, O king. We still wouldn't serve your gods or worship the gold statue you set up."

They were confident that God *could* rescue them but asserted that *even if He didn't*, they still wouldn't serve any other god.

That was all Nebuchadnezzar needed to hear. He insisted the furnace be fired up seven times hotter than usual and ordered the three friends bound hand and foot and thrown inside. The fire was so hot that those who threw them into the furnace were killed by the flames.

And suddenly, the king jumped up from his chair. He saw four men, not three, walking freely around the furnace and said the fourth looked "like a son of the gods" (3:25). He ordered the men released and they walked out "not a hair singed, not a scorch mark on their clothes, not even the smell of fire on them!"

King Nebuchadnezzar was so blown away that he blessed God and ordered that anyone who said anything against God would be torn to pieces along with their homes.

Now this story is very similar to Daniel's in that Shadrach, Meshach, and Abednego were faithful to God, unscathed by their trials, and brought glory to God with their faithful obedience. But something's different here. When these three men were walking in the fire, they weren't alone.

We often feel alone in our trials, don't we? In fact, isolation is one of Satan's best and most effective moves against us. We feel no one else is facing what we are, no one could understand us, no one cares.

But we're *not* alone. God has assured us in Hebrews 13:5, "I'll never let you down, never walk off and leave you." And Jesus promises us in Matthew 28:20, "I'll be with you as you do this, day after day after day, right up to the end of the age."

Again, in Isaiah 41:10-13:

"Don't panic. I'm with you. There's no need to fear for I'm your God. I'll give you strength. I'll help you. I'll hold you steady, keep a firm grip on you. Count on it: Everyone who had it in for you will end up out in the cold—real losers. Those who worked against you will end up empty-handed— nothing to show for their lives. When you go out looking for your old adversaries you won't find them—Not a trace of your old enemies, not even a memory. That's right. Because I, your God, have a firm grip on you and I'm not letting go. I'm telling you, 'Don't panic. I'm right here to help you.'"

Don't believe the lies of the enemy, and of your own heart, that tell you you're alone and that God has left you. Don't for a second embrace the idea that God doesn't hear you or care about the furnace into which you've been thrown.

Instead, we *must* lean into the truth of God's Word. And God's Word says that He's walking with us in the fire, that He hasn't left us and never will. When you feel otherwise, speak God's Word out loud. Say it again and again until it drowns out the darkness.

You are not alone. God is by your side in the fire, and He'll see you through to victory.

PAUL

I quit focusing on the handicap and began
appreciating the gift. It was a case of Christ's
strength moving in on my weakness....And so the
weaker I get, the stronger I become.
—2 Corinthians 12:9-10—

Have you heard of Paul's "thorn in the flesh"? He says
that he asked God to remove it three times but God did
not.

Biblical scholars have debated what Paul might have
been referring to and have suggested it might have been

epilepsy, malarial fever, a speech impediment, or impaired sight. The list is long and the answer impossible to know for sure.

But regardless of what afflicted him, I think we can all understand his frustration and his likely confusion. After all, he was a hero of the faith!

He experienced a radical conversion to Christianity and was now one of the greatest evangelists and missionaries of his age, and really, of...ever. I mean, he wrote a large portion of the Bible for crying out loud! And in return for his dedication, he was imprisoned, beaten, whipped, and stoned by the very people he fought to save.

Surely, if *anyone* deserved a favor from God, Paul did! And here he was, asking God to take away this affliction, this "handicap" as it's described in the Bible, and God wasn't answering. Or rather, God was answering and His answer was no.

Why wouldn't God just remove the handicap? Jesus healed even *sinners* who asked Him once but God was saying no to a Christian hero who begged three times to be healed. Let's look at what Paul says about it in 2 Corinthians 12:7-10:

> Because of the extravagance of those revelations, and so I wouldn't get a big head, I was given the gift of a handicap to keep me in constant touch with my limitations. Satan's angel did his best to get me down; what he in fact did was push me to my knees. No danger then of walking around high

and mighty! At first I didn't think of it as a gift, and begged God to remove it. Three times I did that, and then he told me,

My grace is enough; it's all you need.
My strength comes into its own in your weakness.

Once I heard that, I was glad to let it happen. I quit focusing on the handicap and began appreciating the gift. It was a case of Christ's strength moving in on my weakness. Now I take limitations in stride, and with good cheer, these limitations that cut me down to size—abuse, accidents, opposition, bad breaks. I just let Christ take over! And so the weaker I get, the stronger I become.

To be honest, this is such an incredible mindset, such an other-worldly way of looking at his trials, that I believe it could have only come from God himself. Paul stopped dwelling on his handicap and focusing his attention and efforts on attaining healing, and began to understand how his weakness allowed God's strength to work within him.

What's our natural human tendency when it comes to our weaknesses? We hide them. We try to fix them.

With my Type A personality, you'd better believe that the second a weakness reveals itself, the moment a need arises, I'm in the details. I'm learning everything I can and creating a to-do list of tasks to work though until the issue is resolved.

But when we strive to take control, who are we taking that control from? God.

Paul was a powerful leader, even before God took hold of his life. But with a stockpile of power and ability and talent and resources, where does God fit into the picture?

Have you ever noticed that we don't usually come to God when we're living high on a mountaintop? When our family, our career, and our health are all looking up, we thank God and appreciate what He's given us but we don't usually depend on Him like we so desperately should. We depend on ourselves and our circumstances.

It's when we've hit rock bottom, when we've reached the end of our abilities and hope, that we turn to God and learn to lean on Him...usually because we have nothing left to give.

And although it's a painful place to be, leaning on God in complete dependence is always a *good* place to be. Paul understood this and embraced his handicap as a connection to God and *His* power and ability and talent and resources.

And when others see God shining through us in the midst of our weaknesses, they'll see him more clearly, and not diluted by the successful image we so often try to portray.

God's grace was sufficient for Paul. It was enough. And it's enough for us too.

Lean into God today. Allow your trial, your weakness, to become His strength...your test, to become a powerful testimony to others.

PETER

Jesus said, "Feed my sheep....Follow me."
—John 21:19—

Peter was one of the first and most famous disciples of Jesus. Before he met Jesus, his name was Simon and he was a fisherman. But Jesus called him into a new occupation, renamed him Peter (or "Rock"), and informed him that he was the rock on which Jesus would build His church (Matthew 16:18).

Peter was there for it all. He heard Jesus preaching and teaching and watched with his own eyes as He cast out demons and healed the sick. He was experiencing first-hand what every Christian since then could only dream of.

But everything changed the night Jesus was crucified. Despite his fierce vow of loyalty, Peter denied knowing Jesus three times in one night, in order to avoid sharing his fate.

At that point, Peter was undoubtedly convinced that his story was over, that he was beyond the reach of God's forgiveness. After all, he had epically failed God Himself.

And he couldn't even try to explain or apologize. Jesus was gone, dead and buried. Talk about unfinished business, a complete inability to tie up loose ends.

What's interesting is that even after Jesus was resurrected and appeared to the disciples twice, Peter couldn't quite seem to let go of his failure. In John 21:3, not knowing what else to do, he declared, "I'm going fishing." He was returning to his old way of life, before Jesus called him.

But when he tried to return to what he knew, he failed at that too, not catching a single fish. That's when he heard a voice from the shore, "Good morning! Did you catch anything for breakfast?" It's almost as if the voice said, "So you're back to fishing. How's that working out for you?" It was Jesus.

He instructed Peter and the others to cast their nets on the other side of the boat and all of a sudden, there were so many fish they could barely bring them in. Peter jumped out of the boat and swam to Jesus on the shore. John 21:15-19 recounts:

After breakfast, Jesus said to Simon Peter, "Simon, son of John, do you love me more than these?"

"Yes, Master, you know I love you."

Jesus said, "Feed my lambs."

He then asked a second time, "Simon, son of John, do you love me?"

"Yes, Master, you know I love you."

Jesus said, "Shepherd my sheep."

Then he said it a third time: "Simon, son of John, do you love me?"

Peter was upset that he asked for the third time, "Do you love me?" so he answered, "Master, you know everything there is to know. You've got to know that I love you."

Jesus said, "Feed my sheep....Follow me."

In that moment, Peter's strength and determination were renewed. Jesus had forgiven him and restored him to the path he was always supposed to be on.

Have you ever felt like Peter? A complete and utter failure, holding your empty nets?

Maybe you've damaged or destroyed relationships, finances, or your health, and you're convinced you've burned all your bridges. Maybe you believe you've failed at your faith one too many times. In those moments, it's tempting to think back to when life felt more comfortable and to try to recreate those circumstances.

But Jesus was never one for comfort zones. He essentially asked Peter, "Do you love Me? Then follow Me. Don't seek the comfort of your old life but trust Me enough to follow Me on a new path." And He's asking us the same question, and posing the same challenge, today.

It comes back to the lesson we learned from Moses, that nothing this world has to offer, including comfort, familiarity, or the things that have worked for us in the past, can provide a complete and lasting solution to our problems. Those are often the things we reach for when we're faced with pain, loss, depression, or anxiety.

And they *do* bring relief! But it's short-lived, always a temporary fix, like a Band-Aid on a bullet wound. The initial relief eventually ends and we're left alone in the dark again.

Jesus alone can bring us *true* comfort, which is why He calls us to step away from the imitators, the God-replacements we can so easily set up in our hearts.

It wasn't an easy thing for Peter to trust Jesus. After all, Jesus was calling him to the very path from which Peter had just fled in fear.

But oh, the things he accomplished for heaven on that path! Later on in Peter's story, his *shadow alone* healed people as it passed over them. He preached in confidence, made fearless by the Holy Spirit, eventually bringing millions to know Jesus through his life and witness.

We will never, ever (ever!) fall far enough that we cannot be forgiven and restored. Just look at Peter.

If your future feels overwhelming today, resist the temptation to return to what is comfortable and familiar. Remind yourself that it's just a temporary fix. Then jump out of your boat and swim hard after the *only* One that has what you need.

EZEKIEL

But I'll make you as hard in your way as they are in theirs. I'll make your face as hard as rock, harder than granite. Don't let them intimidate you. Don't be afraid of them.
—Ezekiel in 3:8-9—

Ezekiel was a prophet to some of the most oppressive recipients in one of the most depressing times for the children of God. This is the start of a great story, right?

It was the sixth century BC invasion of Israel by Babylon and the Israelites were dealing with their loss in a few different ways. Some were in denial, refusing to see and accept their current circumstances. Others could *only* see their negative circumstances, and embraced complete hopelessness and despair.

And here's Ezekiel, living in the middle of them all. He's given a vision by God and can see the whole picture.

He's zoomed out and tuned into God's plan to *use* these circumstances to Israel's advantage, to make them stronger and better for it. But even though *he's* zoomed out to see the bigger picture, he seems to be the only one.

Have you ever been there? God gives you a glimpse of hope for your future, the audacity to think bigger than the valley you're currently walking through, but everyone around you is tearing you down?

They may not even be intentionally tanking your hopes, but depression and anxiety and negativity and hopelessness are *heavy*...and incredibly contagious. How can you shout the truth in the darkness? How can you share your vision with those who are seemingly blind?

That's what Ezekiel was facing. He knew it. God knew it.

And I *love* what God told him in Ezekiel 2:6-8:

> "Don't be afraid of them, son of man, and don't be afraid of anything they say. Don't be afraid when living among them is like stepping on thorns or finding scorpions in your bed. Don't be afraid of their mean words or their hard looks. They're a bunch of rebels. Your job is to speak to them.

Whether they listen is not your concern. They're hardened rebels. Only take care, son of man, that you don't rebel like these rebels."

God understood, didn't He? What it's like to live in the midst of those with heavy, hopeless hearts. Sometimes hopeless people can say and do hurtful things. But God encouraged Ezekiel to take heart and to be careful that he didn't fall into their habits.

He continued to tell Ezekiel in 3:7-9:

"They won't listen to you because they won't listen to me. They are, as I said, a hard case, hardened in their sin. But I'll make you as hard in your way as they are in theirs. I'll make your face as hard as rock, harder than granite. Don't let them intimidate you. Don't be afraid of them."

The heavy hearts of others often feel like stone fortresses, impenetrable and unyielding. But God encouraged Ezekiel that they weren't the only ones that could stand strong and uncompromising, that He would set Ezekiel even stronger in *his* ways.

Have you ever considered that at the same time that people's hopelessness is wearing you down, your hope might be wearing *them* down? That when their negative words are draining you, your positive words are beginning to take root in their heart?

But it's tiring isn't it, to keep speaking God's truth

when it appears no one is receiving it, or might even be opposed to it? God knew that, too.

That's why he told Ezekiel in 3:17, "Son of man, I've made you a watchman for the family of Israel. Whenever you hear me say something, warn them for me." He explains that when a watchman speaks God's truth, people will choose whether they listen or not and their decision is outside of the watchman's control. But at least the watchman can rest in the fact that *he* is serving God by speaking the truth in the darkness.

It's not a very motivating message, is it? Endlessly speaking God's truth in darkness is hard work and can leave you feeling like a broken record.

But (a) *you* are serving and honoring God and His truth, and you are the only person over whom you have 100% control. And (b) you might just be wearing them down with your light! Their hearts are hard, but God promises to set *our* hearts even harder in His truth and light.

Hold on, friend! You might be on the verge of a breakthrough. Take heart today! Keep hope alive in your speech, in your actions, and in your heart, and God will keep you from falling into the darkness.

SAMUEL

No more hunger, no more thirst, no more scorching heat. The Lamb on the Throne will shepherd them, will lead them to spring waters of Life. And God will wipe every last tear from their eyes.
—Revelation 7:16-17—

Samuel was a judge and prophet. God first spoke to him as a child "at a time when the revelation of God was rarely heard or seen" (1 Samuel 3:1). He dependably delivered God's word to the people of Israel from that time on, leaving Paul to list him as one of God's faithful in Hebrews 11.

But his faithfulness didn't spare Samuel from heartache. His own sons chose not to serve God, taking bribes and corrupting justice.

Then the Israelites rejected God as their King in favor of a human king, despite Samuel's repeated warnings. Once again, though Samuel thought they had *finally* reached a place of fully trusting God, they wanted to be "just like all the other nations" (1 Samuel 8:19).

Then Saul, the king Samuel appointed over the people, disobeyed God. So God instructed Samuel to secretly appoint a new king, David.

David became Saul's most faithful servant, slaying Goliath, marrying Saul's daughter, and becoming captain of his bodyguard. But Samuel spent the last years of his life watching Saul hunt David down, attempting to murder him, and even murdering priests who helped him. Samuel had worked so hard his entire life, only to watch those he served act foolishly and dishonor God.

He'll sleep when he's dead, right? Not Samuel! Saul used a witch to call the poor guy back from the dead to ask him a question he had already answered when he was alive.

Sounds like something my kid would do. Or my husband. Just kidding…mostly.

But maybe you feel like Samuel. You've served God faithfully your entire life, but you still haven't been spared loss, heartache, and utter exhaustion.

Unfortunately, we're not promised a life without loss on earth. That life comes in heaven.

Revelation 7:16-17 says that in heaven, there will be "no more hunger, no more thirst, no more scorching heat. The Lamb on the Throne will shepherd them, will lead them to spring waters of Life. And God will wipe every last tear from their eyes."

But that's not here. Not yet. So until that day comes, what can we do?

Samuel reacted to loss by waiting patiently upon the Lord and continuing to serve faithfully, no matter what everyone else around him chose to do and no matter what loss or disappointment he encountered.

He understood that you can do everything right but still suffer loss and complete and utter exhaustion. So he dedicated *his* life to God, prayed for and supported others in doing the same, and left the outcome in God's hands. And because of his patient obedience, an entire nation was brought back into relationship with God.

It's hard to practice patient obedience when you feel like you're the only one, isn't it? You're holding yourself to a higher standard and no one seems to understand or appreciate the value in doing that.

But who will be brought back into relationship with God because of *your* patient obedience? Who will find you in heaven to hug you and tell you that your example and patience and endless prayers made all the difference in their life? I can't wait to find out.

STEPHEN

But Stephen, full of the Holy Spirit, hardly noticed—
he only had eyes for God, whom he saw in all his
glory with Jesus standing at his side.
—Acts 7:55—

Stephen was selected by the congregation, and commissioned by the apostles, to care for the poor so that the disciples could focus their efforts on preaching and teaching the Word of God. The Bible says in Acts 6:8, "Stephen, brimming with God's grace and energy, was doing wonderful things among the people, unmistakable signs that God was among them."

But those opposed to Christianity weren't having it. First, they tried debating and arguing with him. "But they were no match for his wisdom and spirit when he spoke" (Acts 6:10).

Determined to finish him and his work for Christ, they bribed people to tell lies about him, to stir others up against him. But when he was brought before the high council, God caused his face to shine like an angel. They couldn't take their eyes off of him, the evidence of God's anointing on him was so powerful and clear.

The chief priest demanded Stephen defend himself against the accusations, so Stephen recalled biblical history. He spoke of how Abraham accepted God's promise in faith and how Joseph thrived despite his betrayal thanks to God's hand of blessing, and even saved the lives of those who betrayed him. He recalled how Moses was used by God to save the very people who rejected him, and how those same people later rejected the commands of God.

He concluded that even today, they refused to accept God's truth and murdered anyone who tried to speak it. At that point, people lost their minds and were demanding his death. But here's my favorite part, in Acts 7:55, "But Stephen, full of the Holy Spirit, hardly noticed—he only had eyes for God, whom he saw in all his glory with Jesus standing at his side."

Have you ever been betrayed by others? Have they gossiped and told lies about you? Assumed the worst of you and your intentions, despite having no real reason for it?

Stephen "hardly noticed" the false accusations, or the demands for his death, because he was so full of the Holy Spirit and "only had eyes for God." His focus on God didn't result in his being saved from the accusations, or even from the stoning that followed, but it made him immune to them. Even as they were stoning him to death, Stephen prayed that God would forgive them.

So what's the point of focusing on God if it results in your death anyway? This might be the hardest reading of this entire book, the hardest lesson to truly accept, let alone embrace. Stephen's death resulted in three main benefits.

• *It reminds us that God is present in our trials.* When God allowed Stephen to see both Himself and Jesus in the midst of the trial, Stephen knew that he was not alone, although he likely felt alone, surrounded by accusers. And we can understand that we're not alone either. God is aware of what we're going through, He hasn't forgotten us, and He is with us even if/when no one else is.

• *It reminds us to fill ourselves with the Holy Spirit until it pushes out everything else.* Amazingly, Stephen wasn't even troubled by the accusations. How? Why? Because he had filled himself so much with the Holy Spirit that there wasn't room left for anxiety, drama, or anything else. He "only had eyes for God." When we're in the middle of an attack, we are to fill ourselves so much with God and His truths that it pushes everything else, like fear, anxiety, and hopelessness, out of our hearts.

• *It provides a witness to others.* Not only did Stephen's face shine like an angel, but his final words—"Master, don't blame them for this sin."— served as a powerful testimony to his accusers and supporters alike! Do you know who else was in attendance to hear those words? Saul. Saul who would later become the apostle Paul. Stephen's reaction to his trial, the way God allowed him to handle himself, planted a seed in Saul's heart.

In your trial today, work to fill yourself with the Holy Spirit. Read your Bible every day, play worship music in the background whenever possible, attend church regularly, seek out opportunities to fellowship with other believers.

Fill yourself so much with God that nothing else can exist in your heart or mind. Then trust that God will defend you in your trial, and will use it to provide a witness and testimony to others.

Our trials won't always end in victory; that's a hard and unpopular truth. *But* God will always defend us and use our trials for His glory and a greater purpose than we could imagine. We just have to keep focusing our eyes on Jesus.

SAMSON

God's loyal love couldn't have run out, his merciful love couldn't have dried up. They're created new every morning. How great your faithfulness!
—Lamentations 3:22—

Samson possessed legendary strength, given to him by God to serve a holy agenda. This was a guy who ripped a lion apart with his bare hands and killed 1000 men with the jawbone of a donkey.

But he also possessed a legendary weakness for women. Or perhaps love.

Within just four chapters of the Bible, Samson fell for four different women, the last of whom tricked him into revealing the secret to his strength, his hair. She cut his hair while he slept and betrayed him to the Philistines.

Without his strength, they were able to capture him, gouge out his eyes, and put him to work in prison. And then to add insult to injury, they threw a party to celebrate his capture. They dragged blind Samson out of the prison to put him on display at the party, standing him between two pillars of the building.

Samson had hit rock bottom. He had lost his strength, his sight, and now his dignity.

No one would have blamed him if he simply gave up and died at that point. Anyone would have understood. I mean, what possible hope was there for his future?

Instead, Samson prayed. He prayed for God to give him strength just *one* more time and to redeem him from his rock bottom.

And God met him there. He gave Samson the strength to push the pillars on either side of him and collapse the entire building on the Philistines. Judges 16:30 tells us, "He killed more people in his death than he had killed in his life."

Samson's story reminds us that God can work in us and through us despite our weaknesses. God didn't leave Samson when he fell short of his calling and He won't leave us.

Ever feel like you've made the same mistake a hundred times? Maybe you're like Samson, falling in love with all the wrong people. Maybe you keep falling back into the same addictions. Maybe you feel like you just can't move forward and you're losing hope that you ever will.

No matter how many times we fall, the only truth that matters is that *God can turn the tides again*. In fact, our God specializes in redemption.

He took Samson's capture, something that was bad news no matter how you sliced it, and used it to place him in the midst of over 3000 of his enemies, with the opportunity to defeat them all with one push. What a comeback! Who would have ever seen that one coming?!

Psalm 130:7 encourages us, "O Israel, wait and watch for God—with God's arrival comes love, with God's arrival comes generous redemption." And Lamentations 3:19-23:

> I'll never forget the trouble, the utter lostness, the taste of ashes, the poison I've swallowed. I remember it all—oh, how well I remember—the feeling of hitting the bottom. But there's one other thing I remember, and remembering, I keep a grip on hope: God's loyal love couldn't have run out, his merciful love couldn't have dried up. They're created new every morning. How great your faithfulness!

Our God specializes in redemption. His love is new every morning.

So hold on. Don't die at rock bottom, even if everyone

would understand if you did. Instead, *pray.*

Pray now. Call out to God like Samson, asking God to redeem you just one more time. Our God uses rock bottoms as launching pads for miracles.

ELIJAH

He got up, ate and drank his fill, and set out.
Nourished by that meal, he walked forty days and
nights, all the way to the mountain of God.
—1 Kings 19:8—

Have you read the story of Elijah's showdown with the prophets of Baal in 1 Kings 18? After three years of drought, Elijah suggested a challenge—both he and the false prophets would pray to their god for rain and see which one answered.

The other prophets called out to Baal for hours,

shouting and cutting themselves, with no luck. Elijah doused his offering and altar in water three times, then prayed to God, who answered with fire, burning up the offering, wood, stones, dirt, and all of the water surrounding it.

When God showed up as the only true god, Elijah ordered the false prophets be killed. And then, after three years of drought, it rained so hard that people had to flee to safety.

You would think Elijah would be celebrated, right? He brought rain when it was desperately needed and showed himself to be the true prophet of a mighty God.

Instead, Queen Jezebel determined to murder him. She was angry that Elijah ordered her false prophets killed.

So Elijah fled into the desert to escape her. Exhausted, he collapsed under the shade of a lone broom bush and prayed in 1 Kings 19:5, "Enough of this, God! Take my life —I'm ready to join my ancestors in the grave!" And he fell asleep there.

But that wasn't how his story ended. Instead, an angel woke him up, fed him, and told him, "You've got a long journey ahead of you."

Where was he journeying? Straight to the mountain of God. When he arrived, God appeared to him and asked in 19:9, "So Elijah, what are you doing here?"

Elijah answered:

> "I've been working my heart out for the God-of-the-Angel-Armies. The people of Israel have

abandoned your covenant, destroyed the places of worship, and murdered your prophets. I'm the only one left, and now they're trying to kill me."

God gave Elijah his next move and informed him that he *wasn't* the only one left. Even though Elijah *felt* utterly alone, there were, in fact, 7000 others that stood their ground and refused to worship Baal.

Our feelings can lie to us, can't they? In fact, that's one of Satan's most effective techniques for derailing our faith. He tells us that we're all alone, that no one *truly* cares about us or what happens to us, that no one could possibly understand what we're going through, that our family and friends would be better off if we weren't here anymore.

And when we begin to accept those lies as truths, we act on them. We begin to isolate ourselves from others, which makes us feel even more alone, which only further confirms our suspicions that no one really liked us in the first place.

That's why we *have* to get into the presence of God. If Elijah would have stayed in that desert, he never would have learned the truth from God, that there were thousands of others. But when he delivered his concerns directly to God, God's truth cancelled out the enemy's lie.

If you're alone and exhausted in the desert today, *get up*. Keep moving.

But don't just keep moving through the motions. Move your feet, one step at a time if necessary, straight into God's presence.

PEACE IN THE VALLEY

Don't sit in your own head, replaying the details of your trial over and over again. Spell out your concerns *before God*. Hear the truth directly from Him, not from your own mind, not from well-meaning family or friends.

Listen as God gives you your next move and reassures you that you're not alone, no matter how alone you feel.

Go now. Climb the mountain. God will meet you there.

ELISHA

He took Elijah's cloak—all that was left of Elijah!—and
hit the river with it, saying, "Now where is the God of
Elijah? Where is he?" When he struck the water, the
river divided and Elisha walked through.
—2 Kings 2:14—

Elisha was the prophet that Elijah anointed to succeed
him. Talk about some big shoes to fill! Elijah delivered
deadly accurate prophesies, performed incredible miracles,
and was the most famous prophet of his time.

Elisha was feeling the pressure to live up to Elijah's

reputation. He wasn't ready to lose Elijah, to take his place. Not now. Not yet.

On the day Elijah was to be taken up in a whirlwind to heaven, he repeatedly attempted to leave Elisha behind him. But Elisha repeated over and over, "Not on your life! I'm not letting you out of my sight!" Although he knew that God was going to take Elijah that day, he held on for dear life.

But then Elijah was taken, swept up to heaven in a chariot of fire. It was the time Elisha had been dreading most since he was first anointed by Elijah.

What did he do? How did he respond?

He knew it would happen eventually but he still didn't feel ready. Would he have ever felt ready?

It reminds me of the time before my husband and I became parents. We would have liked to be parents but we didn't feel ready. We needed more money in our paychecks and more saved up in the bank, a better support system, a bigger house, we told ourselves.

It's important to prepare to become a parent, just as it was important for Elisha to learn everything he could from Elijah. Elisha was an incredibly diligent student. But at some point, ready or not, you have to take the leap, don't you?

We prepared as much as we possibly could to become parents and then God met us the rest of the way. In fact, He knew the areas we had neglected, that we didn't even realize we needed to be good parents to our daughter, and developed those as well. We had to prepare and then jump.

Elisha prepared and when he lost the thing he feared losing most, he jumped. He could have watched Elijah ascend to heaven and then returned to farming, to his original career. It was comfortable and familiar, something at which he knew he could succeed.

Instead, Elisha jumped. Second Kings 2:12-14 tells us:

> When he could no longer see anything, he grabbed his robe and ripped it to pieces. Then he picked up Elijah's cloak that had fallen from him, returned to the shore of the Jordan, and stood there. He took Elijah's cloak—all that was left of Elijah!—and hit the river with it, saying, "Now where is the God of Elijah? Where is he?" When he struck the water, the river divided and Elisha walked through.

Elisha ripped his robe in angst. Of course, he lost his mentor and likely his best friend.

But then he made his decision. Elisha jumped.

Sometimes the things we fear most, happen. No matter how tight our grip, no matter how closely we follow, we lose the people and the things we love most.

Maybe you're there today. You've lost a loved one, a career, or something else you weren't ready to lose. Maybe you feel like Elisha, alone in a field, clinging to whatever you have left, like Elisha clinging to Elijah's cloak.

The question is, how will we respond? Will we seek comfort in the familiar? Will we reject the calling of God and return to our old ways? Or will we jump?

What's interesting is that even though Elisha *felt* alone in that moment, he had an audience. The Bible says that a group of prophets had followed Elijah and Elisha and were watching from afar. They witnessed Elijah being taken away and watched Elisha as he decided his next move.

And when they saw Elisha divide the river and walk through they said, "The spirit of Elijah lives in Elisha!" Whether Elisha intended it or not, his decision to jump served as a testimony to God's power and grace.

Others are watching us as we walk through this valley and face loss. And though they may not be believers, they likely believe Proverbs 24:10, "If you fall to pieces in a crisis, there wasn't much to you in the first place."

Your conscious decision to jump will not only strengthen your *own* faith but also the faith of those watching. Who will you inspire? Whose life will you change when they witness your faith in action?

It's scary, you weren't ready yet, but it's here. It's now. And it's not going anywhere. So let's jump together and see where God lands us.

JEREMIAH

We know how troubles can develop passionate
patience in us, and how that patience in turn forges
the tempered steel of virtue, keeping us alert for
whatever God will do next. In alert expectancy such
as this, we're never left feeling shortchanged.
—Romans 5:3-5—

Do you remember when we talked about the people of
Judah in Babylonian exile? And how false prophets
promised they'd return home soon but a true prophet told
them they'd return home in "seventy years...and not a day

before"? Guess what lucky guy got to deliver that unpopular message? Jeremiah!

I love the showdown he had with a false prophet in the temple, in front of all the priests and people there. The false prophet, Hananiah, delivered a prophesy that the people would be delivered from their exile in two years.

I can only imagine that the people listening might have cheered, or at least supported and agreed with Hananiah. Who wouldn't be happy to receive such an encouraging message?

And then there was Jeremiah. (Insert sad trombone slide.) Jeremiah 28:5-9 tells us:

> Prophet Jeremiah stood up to prophet Hananiah in front of the priests and all the people who were in God's Temple that day. Prophet Jeremiah said, "Wonderful! Would that it were true—that God would validate your preaching by bringing the Temple furnishings and all the exiles back from Babylon. But listen to me, listen closely. Listen to what I tell both you and all the people here today: The old prophets, the ones before our time, preached judgment against many countries and kingdoms, warning of war and disaster and plague. So any prophet who preaches that everything is just fine and there's nothing to worry about stands out like a sore thumb. We'll wait and see. If it happens, it happens—and then we'll know that God sent him."

Jeremiah understood that sometimes God's plans aren't what we want to hear but that doesn't change the fact that they're God's plans. He also knew that the message Hananiah was prophesying wasn't biblical. It didn't line up with God's Word.

There are a lot of popular "Christian" messages floating around these days like, "God wants to make us all successful, go-getting millionaires!" or "We can avoid trials in life if we just have enough faith!"

And those messages sound incredible! But none of them are biblical.

What does the Bible say about trials? Romans 5:3-5 provides perspective for when (not if) we're stuck in the trenches:

> There's more to come: We continue to shout our praise even when we're hemmed in with troubles, because we know how troubles can develop passionate patience in us, and how that patience in turn forges the tempered steel of virtue, keeping us alert for whatever God will do next. In alert expectancy such as this, we're never left feeling shortchanged. Quite the contrary—we can't round up enough containers to hold everything God generously pours into our lives through the Holy Spirit!

The Bible tells us that we are not exempt from facing challenges. We live in a fallen world where trials are a given, Christian or not.

But...but. There's hope in our trials.

Because we're not alone in them. God is using them to develop perseverance, character, and hope in our hearts. He's making us stronger for them.

I recently attended a retreat with some church leaders, where something one of the speakers said really struck me. He explained that God is capable of taking us from point A to point B, performing a miracle that transports us directly from our lowest valley to a mountaintop, but He rarely does. Why? Because what we gain between those two points is invaluable.

I've personally found that when everything is going well in my life—my family, my career, my health, my success—I don't grow much in my faith. My periods of greatest spiritual growth and maturity have all developed in valleys, not on mountaintops.

And that's not to say there isn't hope. Though Jeremiah's message was unpopular at the time, he followed it up with one of the most encouraging and life-giving Bible verses there is in Jeremiah 29:11:

> "As soon as Babylon's seventy years are up and not a day before, I'll show up and take care of you as I promised and bring you back home. I know what I'm doing. I have it all planned out—plans to take care of you, not abandon you, plans to give you the future you hope for."

JEREMIAH

We may be in a valley now and to be honest, we may be here a while. But this is not how our story ends.

God promises the future we hope for and He promises that our trials will only make us stronger. When our bright future finally arrives, we'll be ready for it, and better for it.

GIDEON

"God is with you, O mighty warrior!"
—Judges 6:12—

When I was writing this devotional, praying over every page, every sentence, every word, I felt lead to jot down Gideon's name. And to be honest, I wasn't convinced.

I've read Gideon's story and heard it preached from a pulpit and I just wasn't sure that he was the right guy for the job. I mean, was he truly living in darkness? Could he relate to those of us walking through the valley?

But as I sat down to write about him, it was like his story brought everything together, like his testimony brought it all into focus.

See, Gideon was alive at a time when Midianites were badly dominating God's people. They were destroying their crops (essentially starving the Israelites) and causing them to hide out in mountain caves in fear for their lives.

When we first meet Gideon, he's threshing wheat in the winepress. Wheat should be threshed in the open air but Gideon was hiding from the Midianities. A real warrior, right?

As he's threshing wheat, an angel approaches him and says, "God is with you, O mighty warrior!" Psh! Gideon was sure the angel was mistaken in Judges 6:13-16:

> Gideon replied, "With *me*, my master? If God is with us, why has all this happened to us? Where are all the miracle-wonders our parents and grandparents told us about, telling us, 'Didn't God deliver us from Egypt?' The fact is, God has nothing to do with us—he has turned us over to Midian."

> But God faced him directly: "Go in this strength that is yours. Save Israel from Midian. Haven't I just sent you?"

> Gideon said to him, "*Me*, my master? How and with what could I ever save Israel? Look at me. My

clan's the weakest in Manasseh and I'm the runt of the litter."

God said to him, "I'll be with you. Believe me, you'll defeat Midian as one man."

Have you ever felt like Gideon? I can't even count the number of people I've talked to with similar sentiments. "If God is with us, why has all this happened to us?...God has nothing to do with us."

And how does God respond? "I'm sending *you*."

On his first mission, God told Gideon to chop down his father's Baal altar and use it as firewood to offer a sacrifice to God. But Gideon was so afraid of how his family and neighbors would react that he did it in secret at night.

On his next mission, a call to battle, he was growing in confidence in God. But he still insisted that God provide *two* supernatural signs to him that he would win the battle, before he would dive in.

God provided him with not two but three signs that victory was his, so that Gideon could feel "bold and confident." And in that battle, God lead Gideon to defeat 135,000 Midianite soldiers with just 300 men.

There's a lot more to Gideon's story if you'd like to read about him but today we're focusing on his calling. At a time when Gideon was certain God had abandoned the entire country, at the moment he was hiding in the winepress to thresh wheat, God called *him* to battle.

When we're walking through the valley, we often ask

God when we'll be delivered. We're waiting in a hellish purgatory for something to change, for God's hand to move. But have you ever considered that God might be calling *you*?

Like Gideon, you might not feel like a mighty warrior. The good news is that you don't have to be. In fact, God purposely reduced Gideon's army from 32,000 to just 300, so they would know for certain it was God working through them and not their own size or strength.

Wherever you are today, even if you're hiding in fear like Gideon, ask God if he's calling *you*, too. "God is with you, O mighty warrior!"

To be honest, I don't always like to take charge. I tend to be the organizer of all things for my family and it's exhausting. If you asked me who I am, I might call myself Tired, Worn Out, Overwhelmed, Underqualified, Introvert.

But God doesn't speak to how I feel. Emotions lie. God doesn't. That's why He speaks to who I *am*. And I *am* a Mighty Warrior.

Please don't allow your fear to define your self-image. Don't allow your current circumstances to place a label on you that's just not true.

God calls you Valuable, Transformed, Redeemed, Accepted, Triumphant, Mighty Warrior. Ask Him for your mission, for your calling.

Joseph's false accusations felt like a punishment but they were actually lining him up to step into a position second only to a king. Daniel's exile to Babylon was a dark and hopeless valley to face but God used it to bring an entire country to serve and worship the Lord. Like Esther, you may have arrived in your position today "for such a time as this" (Esther 4:14).

So rise up, Mighty Warrior! Accept your identity in Christ and march forward into the light, as the sun rises on your new beginning.

About the Author

Deb Preston has known God and been reading and studying His Word for over 30 years, through both personal and classroom study. She always wanted to be a writer as a child but fell back on a more stable career when she gained her BS in Exercise Physiology at Oral Roberts University and her MA in Management and Leadership at Liberty University.

But God was always calling her back to writing, as both a career and ministry. She launched DebPreston.com in 2017, where she regularly writes about faith, family, community, and health, as an answer to that call.

After spending several heart-breaking years in her own valley, Deb woke up one day with the words of *Peace in the Valley* burning in her heart. For months, she prayed over and poured out every word onto paper, strongly compelled to write tirelessly until the final manuscript was submitted for printing. She firmly believes that if you're holding this book, these words were intended specifically for you.

Also by Deb Preston

FAITH-BASED BOOKS

Learning on the Fly and Laughing Till I Cry: A Journal of Mothering My Daughter From Ages One to Seven, 2023

Word-ly Women: A Small Group Study Guide, 2021

CONTRIBUTING AUTHOR

So God Made a Mother: Tender, Proud, Strong, Faithful, Known, Beautiful, Worthy, and Unforgettable - Just Like You, 2023

CHILDREN'S BOOKS

Girls Can, 2023

Bodies Can, 2024